50 Cookies, Cakes & More Recipes

By: Kelly Johnson

Table of Contents

- Chocolate Chip Cookies
- Oatmeal Raisin Cookies
- Peanut Butter Cookies
- Sugar Cookies
- Snickerdoodles
- Double Chocolate Cookies
- Macadamia Nut Cookies
- Shortbread Cookies
- Gingerbread Cookies
- Almond Biscotti
- Fortune Cookies
- Thumbprint Cookies
- Meringue Cookies
- Linzer Cookies
- Butter Cookies
- Molasses Cookies
- Chocolate Crinkle Cookies
- Matcha Green Tea Cookies
- Red Velvet Cookies
- Lemon Cookies
- Brownies
- Blondies
- Chocolate Lava Cake
- Classic Cheesecake
- New York-Style Cheesecake
- Japanese Cotton Cheesecake
- Carrot Cake
- Red Velvet Cake
- Black Forest Cake
- Tiramisu
- Tres Leches Cake
- Pound Cake
- Angel Food Cake
- Chiffon Cake
- Butter Cake

- Molten Chocolate Cake
- Strawberry Shortcake
- Coconut Cake
- Funfetti Cake
- German Chocolate Cake
- Banana Bread
- Apple Pie
- Pecan Pie
- Lemon Tart
- Chocolate Mousse
- Éclairs
- Cream Puffs
- Macarons
- Cannoli
- Baklava

Chocolate Chip Cookies

Ingredients:

- 1 cup butter (softened)
- 1 cup brown sugar
- ½ cup white sugar
- 2 eggs
- 1 tsp vanilla extract
- 2 ¼ cups all-purpose flour
- 1 tsp baking soda
- ½ tsp salt
- 2 cups chocolate chips

Instructions:

1. Preheat oven to 350°F (175°C).
2. Cream butter, brown sugar, and white sugar together.
3. Beat in eggs and vanilla.
4. Mix flour, baking soda, and salt, then add to wet ingredients.
5. Stir in chocolate chips.
6. Scoop onto a baking sheet and bake for 10-12 minutes.

Oatmeal Raisin Cookies

Ingredients:

- 1 cup butter (softened)
- 1 cup brown sugar
- ½ cup white sugar
- 2 eggs
- 1 tsp vanilla extract
- 1 ½ cups all-purpose flour
- 1 tsp baking soda
- ½ tsp cinnamon
- 3 cups rolled oats
- 1 cup raisins

Instructions:

1. Preheat oven to 350°F (175°C).
2. Cream butter, brown sugar, and white sugar together.
3. Beat in eggs and vanilla.
4. Mix flour, baking soda, and cinnamon, then add to wet ingredients.
5. Stir in oats and raisins.
6. Scoop onto a baking sheet and bake for 10-12 minutes.

Peanut Butter Cookies

Ingredients:

- 1 cup peanut butter
- ½ cup butter (softened)
- 1 cup sugar
- ½ cup brown sugar
- 1 egg
- 1 tsp vanilla extract
- 1 ½ cups all-purpose flour
- 1 tsp baking soda
- ½ tsp salt

Instructions:

1. Preheat oven to 350°F (175°C).
2. Cream peanut butter, butter, and sugars together.
3. Beat in egg and vanilla.
4. Mix flour, baking soda, and salt, then add to wet ingredients.
5. Roll into balls, press with a fork, and bake for 10-12 minutes.

Sugar Cookies

Ingredients:

- 1 cup butter (softened)
- 1 cup sugar
- 1 egg
- 1 tsp vanilla extract
- 2 ½ cups all-purpose flour
- 1 tsp baking powder
- ½ tsp salt

Instructions:

1. Preheat oven to 350°F (175°C).
2. Cream butter and sugar together.
3. Beat in egg and vanilla.
4. Mix flour, baking powder, and salt, then add to wet ingredients.
5. Roll out dough, cut into shapes, and bake for 8-10 minutes.

Snickerdoodles

Ingredients:

- 1 cup butter (softened)
- 1 ½ cups sugar
- 2 eggs
- 2 ¾ cups all-purpose flour
- 1 tsp baking soda
- ½ tsp salt
- 1 tsp cream of tartar
- 2 tbsp sugar + 1 tsp cinnamon (for coating)

Instructions:

1. Preheat oven to 375°F (190°C).
2. Cream butter and sugar together, then beat in eggs.
3. Mix flour, baking soda, salt, and cream of tartar.
4. Roll dough into balls, coat in cinnamon-sugar, and bake for 10-12 minutes.

Double Chocolate Cookies

Ingredients:

- 1 cup butter (softened)
- 1 cup sugar
- ½ cup brown sugar
- 2 eggs
- 1 tsp vanilla extract
- 2 cups all-purpose flour
- ½ cup cocoa powder
- 1 tsp baking soda
- ½ tsp salt
- 2 cups chocolate chips

Instructions:

1. Preheat oven to 350°F (175°C).
2. Cream butter, sugar, and brown sugar together.
3. Beat in eggs and vanilla.
4. Mix flour, cocoa powder, baking soda, and salt, then add to wet ingredients.
5. Stir in chocolate chips.
6. Scoop onto a baking sheet and bake for 10-12 minutes.

Macadamia Nut Cookies

Ingredients:

- 1 cup butter (softened)
- ¾ cup sugar
- ¾ cup brown sugar
- 2 eggs
- 1 tsp vanilla extract
- 2 ½ cups all-purpose flour
- 1 tsp baking soda
- ½ tsp salt
- 1 cup white chocolate chips
- 1 cup macadamia nuts (chopped)

Instructions:

1. Preheat oven to 350°F (175°C).
2. Cream butter, sugar, and brown sugar together.
3. Beat in eggs and vanilla.
4. Mix flour, baking soda, and salt, then add to wet ingredients.
5. Stir in white chocolate chips and macadamia nuts.
6. Scoop onto a baking sheet and bake for 10-12 minutes.

Shortbread Cookies

Ingredients:

- 1 cup butter (softened)
- ½ cup sugar
- 2 cups all-purpose flour
- ½ tsp vanilla extract

Instructions:

1. Preheat oven to 325°F (165°C).
2. Cream butter and sugar together.
3. Mix in flour and vanilla until dough forms.
4. Roll out dough, cut into shapes, and bake for 12-15 minutes.

Gingerbread Cookies

Ingredients:

- ¾ cup butter (softened)
- ¾ cup brown sugar
- ½ cup molasses
- 1 egg
- 3 cups all-purpose flour
- 1 tsp baking soda
- 1 tbsp ground ginger
- 1 tsp cinnamon
- ½ tsp cloves
- ½ tsp salt

Instructions:

1. Preheat oven to 350°F (175°C).
2. Cream butter, sugar, and molasses together.
3. Beat in egg.
4. Mix flour, baking soda, and spices, then add to wet ingredients.
5. Roll out dough, cut into shapes, and bake for 8-10 minutes.

Almond Biscotti

Ingredients:

- 1 ¾ cups all-purpose flour
- ¾ cup sugar
- 1 tsp baking powder
- ½ tsp salt
- 2 eggs
- 1 tsp vanilla extract
- 1 cup almonds (chopped)

Instructions:

1. Preheat oven to 350°F (175°C).
2. Mix flour, sugar, baking powder, and salt.
3. Beat in eggs and vanilla until dough forms.
4. Fold in almonds and shape dough into a log.
5. Bake for 25 minutes, then cool and slice.
6. Bake slices for another 10-12 minutes until crisp.

Fortune Cookies

Ingredients:

- 2 egg whites
- ½ cup sugar
- ½ cup all-purpose flour
- ½ tsp vanilla extract
- 1 tbsp water

Instructions:

1. Preheat oven to 350°F (175°C).
2. Beat egg whites and sugar until frothy.
3. Stir in flour, vanilla, and water.
4. Spoon small circles of batter onto a baking sheet.
5. Bake for 8-10 minutes until edges brown.
6. Quickly fold each cookie in half with a paper fortune inside.

Thumbprint Cookies

Ingredients:

- 1 cup butter (softened)
- ½ cup sugar
- 2 cups all-purpose flour
- ½ tsp vanilla extract
- ½ cup jam (strawberry, raspberry, or apricot)

Instructions:

1. Preheat oven to 350°F (175°C).
2. Cream butter and sugar together.
3. Mix in flour and vanilla until dough forms.
4. Roll dough into small balls and place on a baking sheet.
5. Press a thumb into each ball to create a well, then fill with jam.
6. Bake for 10-12 minutes until golden.

Meringue Cookies

Ingredients:

- 3 egg whites
- ¾ cup sugar
- ½ tsp vanilla extract
- ¼ tsp cream of tartar

Instructions:

1. Preheat oven to 225°F (110°C).
2. Beat egg whites and cream of tartar until foamy.
3. Gradually add sugar while beating until stiff peaks form.
4. Mix in vanilla.
5. Pipe or spoon onto a baking sheet.
6. Bake for 1 ½ to 2 hours until crisp.

Linzer Cookies

Ingredients:

- 1 cup butter (softened)
- ½ cup sugar
- 1 egg yolk
- 1 tsp vanilla extract
- 2 cups all-purpose flour
- ½ tsp cinnamon
- ½ cup almond flour
- ½ cup raspberry jam
- Powdered sugar (for dusting)

Instructions:

1. Preheat oven to 350°F (175°C).
2. Cream butter and sugar together.
3. Mix in egg yolk and vanilla.
4. Combine flour, cinnamon, and almond flour, then add to wet ingredients.
5. Roll out dough and cut into shapes, cutting a smaller hole in half of the cookies.
6. Bake for 10-12 minutes.
7. Spread jam on whole cookies, place cut-out cookies on top, and dust with powdered sugar.

Butter Cookies

Ingredients:

- 1 cup butter (softened)
- ¾ cup sugar
- 1 egg
- 2 cups all-purpose flour
- ½ tsp vanilla extract

Instructions:

1. Preheat oven to 350°F (175°C).
2. Cream butter and sugar together.
3. Beat in egg and vanilla.
4. Mix in flour until dough forms.
5. Pipe or shape into rounds and bake for 10-12 minutes.

Molasses Cookies

Ingredients:

- ¾ cup butter (softened)
- 1 cup brown sugar
- ¼ cup molasses
- 1 egg
- 2 ¼ cups all-purpose flour
- 1 tsp baking soda
- 1 tsp cinnamon
- ½ tsp ginger
- ½ tsp cloves
- ½ tsp salt

Instructions:

1. Preheat oven to 375°F (190°C).
2. Cream butter and sugar together.
3. Beat in molasses and egg.
4. Mix flour, baking soda, spices, and salt, then add to wet ingredients.
5. Roll dough into balls, coat in sugar, and bake for 10-12 minutes.

Chocolate Crinkle Cookies

Ingredients:

- 1 cup sugar
- ½ cup vegetable oil
- 2 eggs
- 1 tsp vanilla extract
- 1 cup all-purpose flour
- ½ cup cocoa powder
- 1 tsp baking powder
- ½ tsp salt
- ½ cup powdered sugar (for rolling)

Instructions:

1. Preheat oven to 350°F (175°C).
2. Mix sugar, oil, eggs, and vanilla together.
3. Combine flour, cocoa powder, baking powder, and salt, then mix into wet ingredients.
4. Chill dough for 1 hour.
5. Roll dough into balls, coat in powdered sugar, and bake for 10-12 minutes.

Matcha Green Tea Cookies

Ingredients:

- 1 cup butter (softened)
- ¾ cup sugar
- 1 egg yolk
- 2 cups all-purpose flour
- 1 tbsp matcha powder

Instructions:

1. Preheat oven to 350°F (175°C).
2. Cream butter and sugar together.
3. Mix in egg yolk.
4. Combine flour and matcha, then add to wet ingredients.
5. Shape into small rounds and bake for 10-12 minutes.

Red Velvet Cookies

Ingredients:

- ½ cup butter (softened)
- ¾ cup sugar
- 1 egg
- 1 tsp vanilla extract
- 1 ½ cups all-purpose flour
- 1 tbsp cocoa powder
- 1 tsp baking soda
- ½ tsp salt
- 1 tbsp red food coloring
- ½ cup white chocolate chips

Instructions:

1. Preheat oven to 350°F (175°C).
2. Cream butter and sugar together.
3. Beat in egg, vanilla, and food coloring.
4. Mix flour, cocoa powder, baking soda, and salt, then add to wet ingredients.
5. Stir in white chocolate chips.
6. Scoop onto a baking sheet and bake for 10-12 minutes.

Lemon Cookies

Ingredients:

- ½ cup butter (softened)
- ¾ cup sugar
- 1 egg
- 1 tsp vanilla extract
- Zest of 1 lemon
- 1 ½ cups all-purpose flour
- ½ tsp baking soda
- ½ tsp salt
- 1 tbsp lemon juice

Instructions:

1. Preheat oven to 350°F (175°C).
2. Cream butter and sugar together.
3. Beat in egg, vanilla, and lemon zest.
4. Mix flour, baking soda, and salt, then add to wet ingredients.
5. Stir in lemon juice.
6. Scoop onto a baking sheet and bake for 10-12 minutes.

Brownies

Ingredients:

- 1 cup butter (melted)
- 1 cup sugar
- ½ cup brown sugar
- 2 eggs
- 1 tsp vanilla extract
- ¾ cup cocoa powder
- 1 cup all-purpose flour
- ½ tsp baking powder
- ½ tsp salt

Instructions:

1. Preheat oven to 350°F (175°C).
2. Mix melted butter, sugar, and brown sugar together.
3. Beat in eggs and vanilla.
4. Mix cocoa powder, flour, baking powder, and salt, then add to wet ingredients.
5. Pour into a greased pan and bake for 25-30 minutes.

Blondies

Ingredients:

- ½ cup butter (melted)
- 1 cup brown sugar
- 1 egg
- 1 tsp vanilla extract
- 1 cup all-purpose flour
- ½ tsp baking powder
- ½ tsp salt
- ½ cup chocolate chips or nuts (optional)

Instructions:

1. Preheat oven to 350°F (175°C).
2. Mix melted butter and brown sugar together.
3. Beat in egg and vanilla.
4. Mix flour, baking powder, and salt, then add to wet ingredients.
5. Stir in chocolate chips or nuts if using.
6. Pour into a greased pan and bake for 20-25 minutes.

Chocolate Lava Cake

Ingredients:

- ½ cup butter
- 4 oz dark chocolate (chopped)
- 2 eggs
- 2 egg yolks
- ¼ cup sugar
- 2 tbsp all-purpose flour
- Butter and cocoa powder (for greasing ramekins)

Instructions:

1. Preheat oven to 425°F (220°C). Grease ramekins with butter and dust with cocoa powder.
2. Melt butter and chocolate together, stirring until smooth.
3. In a separate bowl, whisk eggs, egg yolks, and sugar until pale.
4. Fold in melted chocolate, then gently mix in flour.
5. Divide into ramekins and bake for 10-12 minutes until edges are set but the center is soft.
6. Let cool for 1 minute, then invert onto plates and serve warm.

Classic Cheesecake

Ingredients:

- 2 cups graham cracker crumbs
- ½ cup butter (melted)
- 3 (8 oz) packages cream cheese (softened)
- 1 cup sugar
- 3 eggs
- 1 tsp vanilla extract
- ½ cup sour cream

Instructions:

1. Preheat oven to 325°F (163°C). Mix graham crumbs with melted butter and press into a springform pan.
2. Beat cream cheese and sugar until smooth. Add eggs one at a time, mixing well.
3. Stir in vanilla and sour cream.
4. Pour filling over crust and bake for 50-60 minutes.
5. Let cool completely before refrigerating for at least 4 hours.

New York-Style Cheesecake

Ingredients:

- 2 cups graham cracker crumbs
- ½ cup butter (melted)
- 4 (8 oz) packages cream cheese (softened)
- 1 ¼ cups sugar
- 3 tbsp all-purpose flour
- 4 eggs
- 1 cup sour cream
- 2 tsp vanilla extract

Instructions:

1. Preheat oven to 325°F (163°C). Press graham cracker crust into a springform pan.
2. Beat cream cheese, sugar, and flour together.
3. Add eggs one at a time, then mix in sour cream and vanilla.
4. Pour filling over crust and bake for 1 hour.
5. Let cool, then chill overnight before serving.

Japanese Cotton Cheesecake

Ingredients:

- 8 oz cream cheese (softened)
- ¼ cup butter
- ½ cup milk
- 6 eggs (separated)
- ⅔ cup sugar
- ¾ cup cake flour
- 2 tbsp cornstarch
- 1 tsp lemon juice

Instructions:

1. Preheat oven to 320°F (160°C). Grease a springform pan and line with parchment paper.
2. Melt cream cheese, butter, and milk together, then let cool.
3. Whisk in egg yolks, then sift in flour and cornstarch.
4. Beat egg whites with sugar until stiff peaks form, then fold into batter.
5. Pour into pan and bake in a water bath for 1 hour.
6. Let cool before removing from the pan.

Carrot Cake

Ingredients:

- 2 cups all-purpose flour
- 2 tsp baking powder
- 1 ½ tsp cinnamon
- ½ tsp salt
- ¾ cup vegetable oil
- 1 cup sugar
- ½ cup brown sugar
- 4 eggs
- 2 tsp vanilla extract
- 2 cups grated carrots
- ½ cup chopped walnuts (optional)

Instructions:

1. Preheat oven to 350°F (175°C). Grease a cake pan.
2. Mix flour, baking powder, cinnamon, and salt.
3. In a separate bowl, whisk oil, sugar, eggs, and vanilla.
4. Stir in carrots and walnuts.
5. Fold dry ingredients into wet ingredients.
6. Bake for 35-40 minutes.
7. Let cool and frost with cream cheese frosting.

Red Velvet Cake

Ingredients:

- 2 ½ cups all-purpose flour
- 2 tbsp cocoa powder
- 1 tsp baking soda
- ½ tsp salt
- 1 cup butter (softened)
- 2 cups sugar
- 4 eggs
- 1 cup buttermilk
- 2 tsp vanilla extract
- 2 tbsp red food coloring
- 1 tsp vinegar

Instructions:

1. Preheat oven to 350°F (175°C). Grease cake pans.
2. Mix flour, cocoa, baking soda, and salt.
3. Beat butter and sugar until fluffy. Add eggs one at a time.
4. Stir in vanilla and food coloring.
5. Alternate adding flour and buttermilk.
6. Stir in vinegar.
7. Divide batter into pans and bake for 30 minutes.
8. Cool and frost with cream cheese frosting.

Black Forest Cake

Ingredients:

- 1 ¾ cups all-purpose flour
- ¾ cup cocoa powder
- 1 ½ tsp baking powder
- ½ tsp baking soda
- 1 cup sugar
- ½ cup vegetable oil
- 2 eggs
- 1 cup buttermilk
- 1 tsp vanilla extract
- 1 can cherry pie filling
- 2 cups whipped cream

Instructions:

1. Preheat oven to 350°F (175°C). Grease cake pans.
2. Mix flour, cocoa, baking powder, and baking soda.
3. Beat sugar, oil, eggs, buttermilk, and vanilla together.
4. Combine wet and dry ingredients.
5. Bake for 30-35 minutes. Let cool.
6. Layer cake with whipped cream and cherries.

Tiramisu

Ingredients:

- 1 cup heavy cream
- 8 oz mascarpone cheese
- ¼ cup sugar
- 2 tsp vanilla extract
- 1 cup espresso (cooled)
- 2 tbsp coffee liqueur (optional)
- 24 ladyfingers
- Cocoa powder (for dusting)

Instructions:

1. Whip cream, mascarpone, sugar, and vanilla until stiff peaks form.
2. Mix espresso and liqueur in a bowl.
3. Dip ladyfingers in coffee mixture and layer with mascarpone cream.
4. Repeat layers, then dust with cocoa powder.
5. Refrigerate for at least 4 hours before serving.

Tres Leches Cake

Ingredients:

- 1 cup all-purpose flour
- 1 ½ tsp baking powder
- ¼ tsp salt
- 5 eggs
- 1 cup sugar
- ⅓ cup milk
- 1 tsp vanilla extract
- 1 can evaporated milk
- 1 can sweetened condensed milk
- ½ cup heavy cream

Instructions:

1. Preheat oven to 350°F (175°C). Grease a cake pan.
2. Mix flour, baking powder, and salt.
3. Beat eggs and sugar until fluffy.
4. Stir in milk and vanilla, then fold in flour mixture.
5. Bake for 30 minutes.
6. Poke holes in cake and pour in mixed milks.
7. Chill and top with whipped cream.

Pound Cake

Ingredients:

- 1 cup butter (softened)
- 2 cups sugar
- 4 eggs
- 1 tsp vanilla extract
- 2 cups all-purpose flour
- ½ tsp baking powder
- ½ cup milk

Instructions:

1. Preheat oven to 350°F (175°C). Grease a loaf pan.
2. Cream butter and sugar together.
3. Beat in eggs one at a time, then mix in vanilla.
4. Alternate adding flour and milk.
5. Bake for 50-60 minutes.

Angel Food Cake

Ingredients:

- 1 cup cake flour
- 1 ½ cups sugar
- 12 egg whites
- 1 tsp cream of tartar
- 1 tsp vanilla extract

Instructions:

1. Preheat oven to 350°F (175°C).
2. Beat egg whites and cream of tartar until foamy.
3. Slowly add sugar while beating until stiff peaks form.
4. Fold in flour and vanilla.
5. Pour into an ungreased tube pan and bake for 35-40 minutes.

Chiffon Cake

Ingredients:

- 2 ¼ cups cake flour
- 1 ½ cups sugar
- 1 tbsp baking powder
- ½ tsp salt
- ½ cup vegetable oil
- 7 egg yolks
- ¾ cup water
- 2 tsp vanilla extract
- 1 tsp lemon zest
- 7 egg whites
- ½ tsp cream of tartar

Instructions:

1. Preheat oven to 325°F (163°C).
2. Sift flour, sugar, baking powder, and salt together.
3. Mix in oil, yolks, water, vanilla, and lemon zest until smooth.
4. Beat egg whites and cream of tartar until stiff peaks form.
5. Gently fold whites into the batter.
6. Pour into an ungreased tube pan and bake for 55-60 minutes.
7. Invert pan and let cool completely before removing.

Butter Cake

Ingredients:

- 1 cup butter (softened)
- 2 cups sugar
- 4 eggs
- 3 cups all-purpose flour
- 1 tbsp baking powder
- ½ tsp salt
- 1 cup milk
- 2 tsp vanilla extract

Instructions:

1. Preheat oven to 350°F (175°C). Grease cake pans.
2. Beat butter and sugar until fluffy.
3. Add eggs one at a time, mixing well.
4. Alternate adding flour, baking powder, and salt with milk.
5. Stir in vanilla and bake for 30-35 minutes.

Molten Chocolate Cake

Ingredients:

- ½ cup butter
- 4 oz dark chocolate (chopped)
- 2 eggs
- 2 egg yolks
- ¼ cup sugar
- 2 tbsp all-purpose flour

Instructions:

1. Preheat oven to 425°F (220°C). Grease ramekins with butter.
2. Melt butter and chocolate together.
3. Whisk eggs, yolks, and sugar until thick.
4. Fold in chocolate and flour.
5. Divide into ramekins and bake for 10-12 minutes.
6. Let cool slightly, then serve warm.

Strawberry Shortcake

Ingredients:

- 2 cups all-purpose flour
- ¼ cup sugar
- 1 tbsp baking powder
- ½ tsp salt
- ½ cup butter (cold, cubed)
- ¾ cup heavy cream
- 1 egg
- 2 cups fresh strawberries (sliced)
- 1 cup whipped cream

Instructions:

1. Preheat oven to 400°F (200°C).
2. Mix flour, sugar, baking powder, and salt.
3. Cut in butter until crumbly.
4. Stir in cream and egg until dough forms.
5. Roll out and cut into rounds. Bake for 15 minutes.
6. Layer shortcakes with strawberries and whipped cream.

Coconut Cake

Ingredients:

- 2 ½ cups all-purpose flour
- 1 tbsp baking powder
- ½ tsp salt
- 1 cup butter (softened)
- 2 cups sugar
- 4 eggs
- 1 cup coconut milk
- 1 tsp vanilla extract
- 1 cup shredded coconut

Instructions:

1. Preheat oven to 350°F (175°C). Grease cake pans.
2. Mix flour, baking powder, and salt.
3. Beat butter and sugar until fluffy. Add eggs one at a time.
4. Alternate adding flour and coconut milk.
5. Stir in vanilla and shredded coconut.
6. Bake for 30-35 minutes.

Funfetti Cake

Ingredients:

- 2 ½ cups all-purpose flour
- 2 ½ tsp baking powder
- ½ tsp salt
- 1 cup butter (softened)
- 1 ¾ cups sugar
- 4 egg whites
- 1 cup milk
- 2 tsp vanilla extract
- ½ cup rainbow sprinkles

Instructions:

1. Preheat oven to 350°F (175°C).
2. Mix flour, baking powder, and salt.
3. Beat butter and sugar until fluffy. Add egg whites.
4. Alternate adding flour and milk.
5. Stir in vanilla and sprinkles.
6. Bake for 30-35 minutes.

German Chocolate Cake

Ingredients:

- 2 cups all-purpose flour
- ¾ cup cocoa powder
- 2 cups sugar
- 1 tsp baking soda
- 1 tsp baking powder
- ½ tsp salt
- 1 cup buttermilk
- ½ cup vegetable oil
- 2 eggs
- 2 tsp vanilla extract

Instructions:

1. Preheat oven to 350°F (175°C). Grease cake pans.
2. Mix flour, cocoa, sugar, baking soda, baking powder, and salt.
3. Add buttermilk, oil, eggs, and vanilla.
4. Pour into pans and bake for 30 minutes.

Banana Bread

Ingredients:

- 2 cups all-purpose flour
- 1 tsp baking soda
- ½ tsp salt
- ½ cup butter (melted)
- ¾ cup brown sugar
- 2 eggs
- 1 tsp vanilla extract
- 3 ripe bananas (mashed)

Instructions:

1. Preheat oven to 350°F (175°C). Grease a loaf pan.
2. Mix flour, baking soda, and salt.
3. In another bowl, mix butter, sugar, eggs, and vanilla.
4. Stir in mashed bananas.
5. Fold in dry ingredients.
6. Bake for 50-60 minutes.

Apple Pie

Ingredients:

- 2 ½ cups all-purpose flour
- 1 cup butter (cold, cubed)
- ½ tsp salt
- 6 tbsp ice water
- 6 cups apples (peeled, sliced)
- ¾ cup sugar
- 2 tbsp flour
- 1 tsp cinnamon

Instructions:

1. Preheat oven to 375°F (190°C).
2. Mix flour, butter, and salt until crumbly.
3. Add ice water to form dough. Chill for 30 minutes.
4. Mix apples with sugar, flour, and cinnamon.
5. Roll out dough, fill with apple mixture, and cover with top crust.
6. Bake for 50 minutes.

Pecan Pie

Ingredients:

- 1 pie crust
- 1 cup corn syrup
- 1 cup brown sugar
- 3 eggs
- 1 tsp vanilla extract
- ¼ cup butter (melted)
- 1 ½ cups pecans

Instructions:

1. Preheat oven to 350°F (175°C).
2. Mix syrup, sugar, eggs, vanilla, and butter.
3. Stir in pecans.
4. Pour into pie crust and bake for 50-55 minutes.

Lemon Tart

Ingredients:

- 1 ¼ cups all-purpose flour
- ½ cup butter (cold, cubed)
- ¼ cup sugar
- 3 tbsp cold water
- ¾ cup lemon juice
- 1 cup sugar
- 3 eggs
- 2 tbsp heavy cream
- 2 tbsp butter

Instructions:

1. Preheat oven to 350°F (175°C).
2. Mix flour, butter, sugar, and water to form a dough.
3. Roll out and press into a tart pan. Bake for 15 minutes.
4. Whisk lemon juice, sugar, eggs, cream, and butter over low heat.
5. Pour into crust and bake for 15 minutes.

Chocolate Mousse

Ingredients:

- 6 oz dark chocolate (chopped)
- 3 tbsp unsalted butter
- 3 eggs (separated)
- 2 tbsp sugar
- ½ tsp vanilla extract
- ½ cup heavy cream

Instructions:

1. Melt chocolate and butter together, then let cool slightly.
2. Whisk egg yolks with sugar and vanilla, then mix into chocolate.
3. In a separate bowl, whip egg whites until stiff peaks form.
4. Fold egg whites into chocolate mixture.
5. Whip heavy cream until stiff, then fold into the mousse.
6. Chill for at least 2 hours before serving.

Éclairs

Ingredients:

For the choux pastry:

- 1 cup water
- ½ cup butter
- 1 cup all-purpose flour
- 4 eggs

For the filling:

- 2 cups heavy cream
- ¼ cup powdered sugar
- 1 tsp vanilla extract

For the chocolate glaze:

- ½ cup dark chocolate (melted)
- ¼ cup heavy cream

Instructions:

1. Preheat oven to 400°F (200°C).
2. Boil water and butter. Stir in flour until dough forms.
3. Remove from heat, add eggs one at a time, mixing well.
4. Pipe onto a baking sheet and bake for 25 minutes.
5. Whip cream, sugar, and vanilla for filling.
6. Slice éclairs, fill with cream, and top with chocolate glaze.

Cream Puffs

Ingredients:

For the pastry:

- 1 cup water
- ½ cup butter
- 1 cup all-purpose flour
- 4 eggs

For the filling:

- 1 ½ cups heavy cream
- ¼ cup powdered sugar
- 1 tsp vanilla extract

Instructions:

1. Preheat oven to 400°F (200°C).
2. Boil water and butter, then mix in flour until dough forms.
3. Remove from heat, add eggs one at a time, mixing well.
4. Drop spoonfuls onto a baking sheet and bake for 25 minutes.
5. Whip cream, sugar, and vanilla, then fill cooled puffs.

Macarons

Ingredients:

- 1 cup almond flour
- 1 ¾ cups powdered sugar
- 3 egg whites
- ¼ cup granulated sugar
- ½ tsp vanilla extract
- Food coloring (optional)

For the filling:

- ½ cup butter (softened)
- 1 cup powdered sugar
- 1 tsp vanilla extract

Instructions:

1. Sift almond flour and powdered sugar together.
2. Whisk egg whites, slowly adding sugar, until stiff peaks form.
3. Fold in dry ingredients and vanilla. Add food coloring if desired.
4. Pipe onto a baking sheet and let sit for 30 minutes.
5. Bake at 300°F (150°C) for 15 minutes.
6. Whip butter, powdered sugar, and vanilla for filling, then sandwich between macarons.

Cannoli

Ingredients:

For the shells:

- 2 cups all-purpose flour
- 2 tbsp sugar
- ¼ tsp salt
- 1 tbsp butter
- ½ cup Marsala wine
- 1 egg
- Oil for frying

For the filling:

- 1 ½ cups ricotta cheese
- ½ cup powdered sugar
- ½ tsp vanilla extract
- ¼ cup mini chocolate chips

Instructions:

1. Mix flour, sugar, salt, and butter.
2. Add wine and egg to form a dough. Let rest for 30 minutes.
3. Roll out and cut into circles. Wrap around cannoli molds and fry until golden.
4. Mix ricotta, sugar, vanilla, and chocolate chips for filling.
5. Fill cooled shells and dust with powdered sugar.

Baklava

Ingredients:

- 1 package phyllo dough
- 1 cup butter (melted)
- 2 cups walnuts or pistachios (chopped)
- ½ cup sugar
- 1 tsp cinnamon

For the syrup:

- 1 cup honey
- ½ cup water
- ½ cup sugar
- 1 tsp lemon juice

Instructions:

1. Preheat oven to 350°F (175°C).
2. Mix nuts, sugar, and cinnamon.
3. Layer phyllo sheets, brushing each with butter, and sprinkle nut mixture every few layers.
4. Cut into squares and bake for 45 minutes.
5. Boil syrup ingredients together, then pour over hot baklava.

www.ingramcontent.com/pod-product-compliance
Lightning Source LLC
LaVergne TN
LVHW081334060526
838201LV00055B/2631